SIGNPOSTS TO HEAVEN

A little book of
everlasting wisdom

SIGNPOSTS
TO
HEAVEN
A little book of
everlasting wisdom

COMPILED BY
John Martin

Hodder & Stoughton
LONDON   SYDNEY   AUCKLAND

British Library Cataloguing Publication Data
A record for this book is available from the British Library

ISBN 0 340 65666 2

Printed and bound in Great Britain
by Clays Ltd, St Ives plc

Hodder and Stoughton
A division of Hodder Headline PLC

CONTENTS

1	The First Word	7
2	The Living World	11
3	Being Human	17
4	Meaning and Proof	26
5	Happiness	35
6	Freedom	41
7	Love and Sex	49
8	Suffering	57
9	Prayer and Spirituality	65
10	Atheism	73
11	God	80

12	Jesus	90
13	The Cross and Resurrection	96
14	The Bible	102
15	The Church	108
16	Other Faiths	113
17	Miracles	117
18	Sin	121
19	Hell	127
20	Heaven	133
21	Endpieces	138
	Acknowledgments	140
	Further Reading	141

1
THE FIRST WORD

A word in season, how good it is

The Book of Proverbs

The inspiration for this book was an experience at a company Christmas party. With wine and good cheer flowing, a colleague turned to me with a question about Christianity. That was my cue. I launched with enthusiasm into a learned answer. I had swatted up on evidences for Christian belief for years. Here was a chance to put my vast knowledge to work.

After a minute and a half I noticed his eyes glazing over. The situation reminded me of the boy who asked his mother: 'How does a train work?' 'Why not ask your father?' came the puzzled reply. 'But,' he wailed, 'I don't want to know that much!'.

A lot of people want to know whether faith offers worthwhile answers to their questions. But they may not be ready to digest encyclopaedia-sized answers.

Hence, this collection of soundbites offers a different starting point. For the believer who is

committed to sharing the faith, I hope it will serve as a valuable resource. For the uncommitted – or even the downright sceptic – I hope it will inspire more steps on a road of discovery.

John Martin

2

THE LIVING WORLD

There simply cannot be a design
without a designer.

William Paley

To suppose that the eye, with so many parts all
working together, could have been formed by
natural selection, seems, I freely confess, absurd
in the highest degree.

Charles Darwin

Much more faith is required to attribute the wonders of our world to the chance collision of floating gases than to accept the existence of an eternal, intelligent, and powerful designer God.

Bill Hybels

I believe in God like I believe in the sun. Not just because I can see him, but because by him I can see everything else.

C.S. Lewis

Choose between the absolute empire of accident and a living, immanent, ever-working God.

Charles Kingsley

All are but part of one stupendous whole,
Whose body Nature is, and God the soul.

Alexander Pope

Only when the last tree is cut down, the last river polluted and the last reef killed, may we understand that we cannot eat money.

Max Henderson

Speak to the earth and it
will teach you.

The Book of Job

It is a sobering thought that the early writings of the Jewish people [The Old Testament] encompass all the basic recommendations of world conservation strategy.

David Bellamy

Beauty is the gift of God.

Aristotle

I said to a tree, speak to me of God.
And the tree blossomed.

An Indian proverb

3

BEING HUMAN

Man's chief end is to glorify God and
enjoy Him for ever.

The Westminster Catechism

[Humans] enjoy such an exalted rank in the nature
of things because [we] bear the image of God.

R.C. Sproul

If Man is not a divinity then Man is a disease. Either he is in the image of God, or else he is the one animal which has gone mad.

G.K. Chesterton

A computer can play music, but it takes a human being to enjoy it.

Anon

I can contribute to my salvation, except the sin from which I have been redeemed.

William Temple

We are only cave men who have lost our cave.

Christopher Morley

We have no non-religious activities; only
religious and irreligious.

C.S. Lewis

Man is the only animal that blushes.
Or needs to.

Mark Twain

When you have a fight with your conscience
and get licked, you win.

Anon

Man's extremity is God's
opportunity.

John R. Mott

Nobody knows the age of the human race,
but all agree that it is old enough to know
better.

Anon

All sin seems much worse in its consequences
than in its intentions.

Reinhold Niebuhr

No man knows how bad he is until
he has tried to be good.

C.S. Lewis

The danger of the past is that men became slaves. The danger of the future is that men may become robots.

Erich Fromm

The trouble with the rat race is that even if you win, you're still a rat.

J. John

What does it benefit a man if he gains the whole world and loses his own soul.

Jesus of Nazareth

Nothing recedes like success.

Walter Winchell

So long as men worship the Caesars and Napoleons, Caesars and Napoleons will arise to make them miserable.

Aldous Huxley

4

MEANING AND PROOF

Those who come to God must believe that he exists and rewards those who seek him.

The Epistle to the Hebrews

Seek not to understand that you might believe, but believe that you may understand.

St Augustine

To believe in God is impossible; not to believe in him is absurd.

Voltaire

If we let ourselves believe that man began with divine grace, that he forfeited this by sin, and that he can only be redeemed by divine grace through the crucified Christ, then we shall find peace of mind never granted to the philosophers.

Blaise Pascal

Religious knowledge is much more demanding than scientific knowledge.

John Polkinghorne

There are three roads to belief: reason, habit, and revelation.

Blaise Pascal

There is only one thing a philosopher can be relied on to do and that's to contradict other philosophers.

William James

Insistence on absolute proof for the existence of God is unreasonable and unrealistic ... A more reasonable requirement is that enough evidence is presented to tip the scales.

Bill Hybels

Life is like playing a violin in public and learning the instrument as one goes on.

Samuel Butler

Science without religion is lame. Religion without science is blind.

Albert Einstein

One person with a belief is equal to a force of ninety nine who have only interests.

John Stuart Mill

Faith is love taking the form
of aspiration.

William E. Channing

Faith is not belief in spite of evidence. It is life in scorn of consequence.

Kirsopp Lake

The trouble with life in the fast lane is that you get to the end in a real hurry.

John Jensen

There is more to life than increasing its speed.

Mahatma Gandhi

I believe because it is
impossible.

Tertullian

Logic, *n*. The art of thinking and reasoning in strict accordance with the limitations and incapacities of the human understanding.

Ambrose Bierce, in *The Devil's Dictionary*

Philosophy is the product
of wonder.

A.N. Whitehead

5

HAPPINESS

A man whose heart is not content is like
a snake who tries to swallow an elephant.

A Chinese proverb

A contented spirit is the sweetness
of existence.

Anon

A bitter heart devours its owner.

African proverb

The only true happiness comes from squandering ourselves for a purpose.

William Cowper

No one was ever heard to say on their deathbed, 'I wish I had spent more time at the office.'

Rob Parsons

We have no more right to consume happiness
without producing it than to consume wealth
without producing it.

George Bernard Shaw

The art of being wise is knowing what
to overlook.

William James

Knowledge of what is possible is the beginning of happiness.

George Santayana

Happiness is a way to travel –
not a destination.

Roy Goodman

Happiness depends, as Nature shows,
less on exterior things than most suppose.

William Cowper

Happiness is like coke – something you get as
a by-product of making something else.

Aldous Huxley

Life is God's great novel.
Let him write it.

Isaac Bashevis Singer

Happiness is a mystery like religion, and should never be rationalised.

> G.K. Chesterton

Perfection has one great defect.
It is apt to be dull.

> W. Somerset Maugham

6

FREEDOM

Where the Spirit of the Lord is
the heart is free.

F.F. Bruce

Freedom ... a universal licence to do good.

Samuel Taylor Coleridge

Having given us free will, God has chosen not to interfere with our chosen direction.

Tony Stone

Man's freedom is freedom to betray God.

Dag Hammarskjold

No person is free who is not master of himself.

Epictetus

When you've robbed a man of everything,
he's no longer in your power – he's free again.

Alexander Solzhenitsyn

Man is born free, and
everywhere is in chains.

Jean-Jacques Rousseau

No-one can be perfectly free
till all are free.

Herbert Spencer

Freedom is an indivisible word. If we want to enjoy it, and fight for it, we must be prepared to extend it to everyone.

Wendell Willkie

The enemies of freedom do not argue; they shout and shout.

Dean Inge

Freedom and not servitude is the cure for anarchy; as religion, not atheism, is the true remedy for superstition.

Edmund Burke

The moment a slave resolves he will not be a slave, his fetters fall.

Mahatma Gandhi

Freedom has a thousand charms to show,
That slaves, howe'er contented, never know.

William Cowper

The creation itself will be set free from its bondage to decay and obtain the glorious liberty of the children of God.

St Paul

For all that has been – Thanks!
For all that shall be – Yes!

Dag Hammarskjold

If morals make you dreary,
depend upon it, they are wrong.

Robert Louis Stevenson

7

LOVE AND SEX

There is no fear in love,
for perfect love casts out fear.

The Epistle of St John

The supreme happiness of life is the con-
viction that we are loved.

Victor Hugo

Happiness is not a destination. It is a method of life.

Burton Hills

Love is nothing less than to wish that person good.

Thomas Aquinas

Love your neighbour and be careful of
your neighbourhood.

John Hay

We can never be the better for our religion
if our neighbour is worse for it.

Anon

There are no illegitimate children,
only illegitimate parents.

Leon Yankwich

Help your brother's boat across, and lo thine
own has reached the shore.

Hindu Proverb

There is no pit so deep that God's love
is not deeper still.

Corrie Ten Boom

There's a thin line between muck-raking and
solid analysis. It's called love.

Jamie Buckingham

What we can do for others is the test of powers; what we can suffer is the test of love.

Brooke Foss Westcott

If you want to be loved,
be lovable.

Ovid

Comfort is to faith in Christ what good sex is to marriage – the result of a successful relationship.

Bruce Wilson

Sex is God's present for us for
our wedding day.

J. John

If the imagination were obedient, the appetites would give us very little trouble.

C.S. Lewis

Herein is love, not that we loved God but that he loved us, and sent his Son.

St John

8

SUFFERING

In everything there is a season ... a time to
be born, a time to die ...

Ecclesiastes

A Christian is someone who shares the sufferings
of God in the world.

Dietrich Bonhoeffer

I do not believe that God directly wills either the act of a murderer, or the incidence of cancer. I believe he allows both to happen in a creation to which he has given the gift of being itself.

John Polkinghorne

'It is God who made the world,' men say. 'It should be he who bears the load.' The Church points to the cross and says, 'He did bear it.'

Alister McGrath

It's men, not God, who produced racks, whips, prisons, slavery, guns, bayonets, and bombs.

C.S. Lewis

Most of our comforts grow up
between our crosses.

Edward Young

It is impossible for the human heart
without crosses and tribulations to think
upon God.

Martin Luther

Jesus did not come to explain away suffering
or remove it. He came to fill it with his
presence.

Milo Chapman

Sorrow is a fruit; God does not allow it to grow on a branch that is too weak to bear it.

Victor Hugo

The deeper the sorrow,
the less tongue it hath.

The Talmud

God loves you. God doesn't want anyone to be hungry or oppressed. He just puts his big arms around everybody and hugs them up against himself.

Norman Vincent Peale

Christ leads me through no darker rooms,
Than he went through before.

Richard Baxter

I believe in the sun, even if it does not shine.
I believe in love, even if I don't feel it.
I believe in God, even if I don't see him.

Written on a wall of the Warsaw Ghetto
by a young Jew

The only cure for suffering is to face it head
on, grasp it around the neck, and use it.

Mary Craig

He who suffers much
will know much.

Greek proverb

9

PRAYER AND SPIRITUALITY

Prayer ... the highest energy of which
the mind is capable.

Samuel Taylor Coleridge

Prayer is conversation with God.

St Clement of Alexandria

You need not cry very loud; he is nearer to us than we think.

Brother Lawrence

Creativity is a form of prayer, and the expression of profound gratitude for being alive.

Ben Okri

Your cravings as a human animal do not become
a prayer just because it is God whom you ask to
attend to them.

Dag Hammarskjold

I used to fight my devils, but now I send
them up with jokes.

Rabbi Lionel Blue

Seven days without prayer makes
one weak.

Allen Bartett

Praying is a dangerous business.
Results do come.

G. *Christie Swain*

The fewer the words, the better
the prayer.

Martin Luther

Much silence has a
mighty noise.

An African proverb

I have lived to thank my God that not all my prayers have been answered.

Jean Ingelow

More things are wrought by prayer than this world dreams of.

Alfred, Lord Tennyson

Pray to God in the storm, but
keep on rowing.

Danish proverb

Work is prayer.

Anon

The wish for prayer is a prayer in itself.

Georges Bernanos

If you are swept off your feet,
it's time to get on your knees.

Frederick Beck

I have so much to do today that I must spend
several hours in prayer before I am able to do it.

John Wesley

10

ATHEISM

The fool has said in his heart
there is no God.

The Psalms

The man who bows down to nothing can
never bear the burden of himself.

Dostoevsky

There are no atheists
in foxholes.

William T. Cummings

The religion of the atheist has a God-shaped blank at its heart.

H.G. Wells

Premise 1. The fact that we do not want something to exist does not mean that it does not exist. Premise 2. Atheists do not want God to exist. Conclusion. God does exist ... Wishful thinking can cut both ways.

Alister McGrath

The worst moment for an atheist is when he is thankful and has nothing to thank.

Dante Gabriel Rosetti

An atheist is someone who has no invisible means of support.

John Buchan (Lord Tweedsmuir)

Every effort to prove there is no God is in itself an effort to reach for God.

Charles Edward Locke

An atheist is a man who believes himself an accident.

Francis Thompson

Man by his constitution is a religious animal; atheism is against not only our reason, but our instincts.

Edmund Burke

Agnosticism solves not but merely shelves
the mysteries of life.

Vincent McNabb

The highest praise of God consists of a denial of
him by the atheist who finds creation so perfect
that it can dispense with the creator.

Marcel Proust

The challenge of atheism is a constant safe-guard against idolatry.

John Macquarrie

Where there is no God
there is no man.

Nikolai Berdeyaev

11

GOD

Ever since the creation of the world God's invisible nature, his eternal power and deity have been clearly perceived in the things that have been made.

St Paul

God cannot be reduced to or explained by anything except himself.

Bruce Wilson

God does not die on the day when we cease to believe in a personal deity, but we die on the day when our lives cease to be illuminated by the steady radiance, renewed daily, of a wonder, the source of which is beyond all reason.

Dag Hammarskjold

A comprehended God is
not a God at all.

Gerhard Tersteegen

To him no high, no low, no great,
no small; he fills, he bounds,
connects and equals all.

Alexander Pope

I could prove God statistically.

George Gallup

A God is simply that whereon the human heart rests with trust, faith, hope and love. If the resting is right, then God is right; if the resting is wrong, then the God, too, is illusory.

Martin Luther

If you will not have God (and he is a jealous God), you should pay your respects to Stalin and Hitler.

T.S. Eliot

Every concept of God is a mere simulacrum; a false likeness, an idol. It could not reveal God himself.

Gregory of Nyssa

If the work of God could be comprehended
by reason, it would no longer be wonderful.

Saint Gregory the Great (Pope Gregory 1)

You are never more yourself than when you
are fully God's.

Tony Stone

The person who feels God to be incomprehensible, unknowable, is the one who knows God.

Richard Rollelt

Belief is a wise wager. Granted that faith cannot be proved, what harm will come to you if you gamble on its truth and it proves false? ... If you gain you gain all; if you lose you lose nothing.

Blaise Pascal

If you aren't as close to God as you once were, you can be certain as to which one of you has moved.

Burton Hills

Sometimes a nation abolishes God, but God is more tolerant.

Herbert V. Prochnow

In the nineteenth century the problem was that God was dead. The problem of the twentieth century is that man is dead.

Erich Fromm

Yesterday I saw a robin let go a worm.
That's like God.

A ten-year-old boy

The hardness of God is kinder than the softness of men, and his compulsion is our liberation.

C.S. Lewis

12
JESUS

For God so loved the world that he gave his only Son, that whoever believes in him should not perish but have everlasting life.

Jesus of Nazareth

Jesus loves me, this I know
for the Bible tells me so.

Traditional

Jesus means 'God saves'.

Alister McGrath

How could the human race go to God if God
did not come to us.

St Irenaeus

Jesus is called 'the image of the invisible God'.
The meaning is that this is God and that God is
like this.

Jurgen Moltmann

Great men have come and gone.
Christ lives on.

Anon

We seek God everywhere, but not seeing him in Christ we find him nowhere.

Martin Luther

There is more hard historical evidence for the person of Jesus than for Julius Caesar.

Tony Stone

Who can deny that Jesus of Nazareth, the incarnate son of the most High God, is the eternal glory of the Jewish race?

Benjamin Disraeli

I believe there is no one lovelier, deeper, and more sympathetic and more perfect than Jesus.

Dostoevski

I have a great need for Christ. I have a great Christ for my need.

Charles Haddon Spurgeon

13

THE CROSS AND RESURRECTION

Crosses are ladders that lead to heaven.

English proverb

He was pierced for our transgressions
He was crushed for our iniquities
the punishment that brought us peace was upon him,
and by his wounds we are healed.

The Prophecy of Isaiah

Christ has turned all
our sunsets into dawns.

St Clement of Alexandria

In the cross of Christ, excess in men is met by
excess in God; excess of evil is met by excess
of love.

Louis Bordaloue

I am the resurrection and the life. He who believes in me, though he were dead, yet shall he live, and whoever lives and believes in me shall never die.

Jesus of Nazareth

If Christ has not been raised, then our preaching is in vain and your faith is in vain ...

St Paul

Christianity is at its essence a resurrection religion. The concept of resurrection lies at its heart. If you remove it, Christianity is destroyed.

John Stott

The Gospels do not explain the resurrection; the resurrection explains the Gospels.

John S. Whale

Jesus is alive. He is able to help us, guide us, and strengthen us. Jesus has defeated death. This life will give way to something even fuller and more wonderful.

John Young

Our Lord has written the promise of the resurrection, not in books alone, but in every leaf in springtime.

Martin Luther

The resurrection tells us that when we die, God can take care of us in just the same way as he took care of Jesus.

David Jenkins

If you bear the cross gladly,
it will bear you.

Thomas à Kempis

14

THE BIBLE

England has two books, the Bible and Shakespeare. England made Shakespeare, but the Bible made England.

Victor Hugo

In the Old Testament the New lies hidden. In the New Testament the Old is laid open.

St Augustine of Hippo

One of the divine qualities of the Bible is this: it does not yield its secrets to the irreverent or censorious.

J.I. Packer

If you want to find the Bible full of contradictions, you'll find a way to do it.

Judson Poling

The devil can cite Scripture for
his purposes.

William Shakespeare

What you bring away from the Bible depends
to some extent on what you carry to it.

Oliver Wendell Holmes

It ain't the parts to the Bible that I don't understand that bother me. It's the parts I do understand.

Mark Twain

All that I have taught of art, everything I have
written, every greatness that has been in any
thought of mine, whatever I have done in my life,
has simply been due to the fact that when I was a
child my mother read me part of the Bible, and
daily made me learn part of it by heart.

John Ruskin

The Old and New Testaments are
the Great Code of Art.

William Blake

The English Bible, a book which, if everything else in our language should perish,
would alone suffice to show the extent of its
beauty and power.

Thomas Babington Macaulay

Luke is an historian of the first rank. He should be placed along with the very greatest of historians.

Sir William Ramsey

There are 184,590 words in the New Testament. How many of them have questions about their meaning or grammatical sense or interpretation? Answer 400. And none makes any difference in any doctrinal matter.

Bill Hybels

14

THE CHURCH

See how these Christians love
one another.

Tertullian

He cannot have God for his father who
refuses to have the Church for his mother.

St Augustine of Hippo

Christians do not 'believe in the Creeds', but, with the Creeds to help them, they believe in God.

John Young

Sour godliness is the devil's religion.

John Wesley

It is in the process of being worshipped that God communicates his presence to men.

C.S. Lewis

Most people today go to the theatre to be purged and to the church to be entertained.

Elisabeth Templeton

Most people have some sort of religion. At least they know which church they're staying away from.

John Erskine

It is a great mistake to suppose that God is interested only, or even primarily, in religion.

William Temple

Refusing to belong to the Church because its members are imperfect is like refusing food at a restaurant because the chef has a temper and the waiter a mistress.

Bruce Wilson

Christianity has survived Christians for two thousand years now, which from my point of view is evidence that maybe something is going on there.

T-Bone Burnett

The Christian ideal has not been tried and found wanting. It has been found difficult; and left untried.

G.K. Chesterton

16

OTHER FAITHS

I am the way, the truth and the life, no one comes to the Father but by me.

Jesus of Nazareth

And there is salvation in no one else, for there is no other name [Jesus Christ] under heaven that has been given among men by which we must be saved.

St Peter

The one common denominator of all non-Christian faiths is that they believe that a human being is responsible in part or whole for saving himself.

Bill Hybels

God is an infinite circle whose centre is everywhere and whose circumference is nowhere.

St Augustine of Hippo

Theology is a map of spiritual experience. But we must never confuse maps with the reality they represent.

Bruce Wilson

Approach a man of another faith in the spirit of expectancy to find how God has been speaking to him.

Max Warren

The Christian has no other message for the Muslim than Jesus Christ himself.

Stephen Neill

If Christians are as different from others as they ought to be, questions may arise in the minds of those who watch them.

Stephen Neill

16

MIRACLES

Our daily existence is itself
a miracle.

Stuart Penney

Jesus himself was the one convincing and
permanent miracle.

Ian Maclaren

Once you grant that miracles can happen, all the historical evidence ... bids us believe that sometimes they do.

Ronald A. Knox

Miracles are not contrary to the laws of nature, but discoveries of laws of nature that as yet we've been ignorant of.

Lord Soper (Donald Soper)

A miracle ... is not so much a breach of the laws of human nature, but rather a remarkable or exceptional occurrence which brought an undeniable sense of the presence and power of God.

C.H. Dodd

The divine art of the miracle is not an art of suspending the pattern to which events conform, but of feeding new events into that pattern.

C.S. Lewis

If you don't believe in miracles could it be that it's because you have never celebrated the greatest miracle – God's salvation?

Tony Stone

18

SIN

All have sinned and fallen short
of the glory of God.

St Paul

To sin is nothing else than not to render
God his due.

St Anselm

Sin is a squandering of our humanity, a squandering of our most precious values.

Pope John-Paul II

It's not a case of how much we have sinned: it is the fact that we have sinned.

Tony Stone

The trouble with trouble is that it usually starts out as a whole lot of fun.

Anon

There are very few new sins – and it's the old sins that get all the publicity.

Anon

Keep yourself from opportunity and God will
keep you from sins.

Joseph Cats

We can all do good deeds, but very few of
us can think good thoughts.

Cesar Pavese

If I wrote down every thought I have ever thought and every deed I have ever done, men would call me a monster of depravity.

Somerset Maugham

Men never do evil so completely and cheerfully as when they do it from religious convictions.

Blaise Pascal

Character is what you are
in the dark.

D.L. Moody

Many church people have been starched and
ironed. But they have never been washed.

Paul Hovey

19

HELL

The only shoes you're going to stand in on
the day of reckoning are your own shoes.

Bill Hybels

Death is nothing; but to live without
creating, without contributing, is to die daily.

Jamie Buckingham

Ignorance is not bliss.
It is oblivion.

Philip Wylie

Hell exists because God takes people's choices seriously.

Steve Gaukroger

God gives people in eternity an expanded capacity for what they longed for here on earth.

Bill Hybels

The surest road to Hell is the gradual one – the gentle slope, soft underfoot, without sudden turnings, without milestones, without signposts.

C.S. Lewis

Hell is not to love any more.

Georges Bernanos

The wicked often work harder to go to hell
than the righteous do to enter heaven.

Josh Billings

Hell is truth seen too late, duty neglected
in its season.

Tyron Edwards

If someone does not love God it would be callous for God to require them to live eternally in his presence.

Stuart Penney

There is nobody who will go to hell
for company.

George Herbert

Men are not in hell because God is angry with them. They are in wrath and darkness because they have done to the light, which infinitely flows from God, as that man does to the light of the sun who puts out his own eyes.

William Law

20

HEAVEN

In my Father's house are many mansions ...
I go to prepare a place for you. And if I go
to prepare a place for you I will come again
and receive you to myself, that where I am
there you may be also.

Jesus of Nazareth

Aim at heaven and you will get earth thrown in.
Aim at earth and you will get neither.

C.S. Lewis

To see a world in a grain of sand, and a
heaven in a wild flower.

William Blake

The hills and valleys of heaven will be those you now experience, not as a copy as to an original, nor as a substitute for the genuine article, but as the flower to the root, or the diamond to the coal.

C.S. Lewis

Heaven is full of answers to prayers for which no one bothered to ask.

Billy Graham

Though the threads of my life have been knotted, I know, by faith, that on the other side of the embroidery there is a crown.

Corrie Ten Boom

Saint, *n.* a dead sinner revised and edited.

Ambrose Bierce,
from *The Devil's Dictionary*

If you're not allowed to laugh in heaven, I don't want to go there.

Martin Luther

Heaven is perfect. So if you need your hamster in heaven to make it perfect for you, he'll be there!

Ian Knox

Death is the ultimate healing.

Robert Leach

ENDPIECES

Religion is the total response of a man to his environment.

C. A. Coulson

You say religion is a crutch. There's nothing wrong with a crutch if you have a limb that needs a bit of help.

Lord Soper (Donald Soper)

Nothing can harm a good man, either in
life or in death.

Socrates

'Beauty is truth and truth is beauty', – that is all
Ye know on earth and all ye need to know.

John Keats

To be at all is to be religious
more or less.

Samuel Butler

ACKNOWLEDGMENTS

Signposts to Heaven was compiled by a combination of research and inviting contributions from people involved with communicating the Christian faith, including: Robert Leach, Rhena Taylor, Dr Rob Frost, Dr Tony Stone, Stuart Penney, Ian Knox, Canon John Young, Mark Mittleberg, and Rosemary Green.

FURTHER READING

Classic texts making the case for Christianity

C.S. Lewis, *Surprised by Joy* (London, 1955, Bles).
Mere Christianity (London, 1952, Bles).

Francis Schaeffer, *The God Who is There*, in *A Francis Schaeffer Trilogy*, (Leicester, 1990, IVP).

On the significance, life, death and resurrection of Jesus

Bauckham, R., France, R.T., Maggay, M., Stamoolis, J., and Theide, C.P., *Jesus 2000: A Major Investigation into History's Most Intriguing Figure* (Oxford, 1989, Lion).

Marcus Borg, *Jesus a New Vision* (London, 1993, SPCK).

N.T. Wright, *Who Was Jesus?* (London, 1992, SPCK).

Alister McGrath, *Making Sense of the Cross* (Leicester, 1992, IVP).

Leon Morris, *The Apostolic Preaching of the Cross* (Leicester, 1965, IVP).

John Stott, *The Cross of Christ* (Leicester, 1986, IVP).

OTHER USEFUL READING

Steve Chalke, *More Than Meets the Eye* (London, Hodder & Stoughton, 1996).

Russell Chandler, *Understanding the New Age* (Dallas, 1988, Word).

John Polkinghorne, *Quarks, Chaos and Christianity* (London, 1994, SPCK).